what if?

a guide to
improvisational management

what if?

a guide to improvisational management

Kurt Reinhart

Cover and interior design by Alex LaFasto

ISBN 978-0-9825672-0-3

*To Mom and Dad
for letting me explore and act and be and live.*

*To Shey
for thinking I sometimes know what I am talking about
(it's very true).*

*To Kyle, Grace and Sarah
for influencing me.*

Contents

ACKNOWLEDGEMENT

I must acknowledge the main source for this book; the many, many learners I have had the pleasure to train, instruct, consult and with whom I have shared time. All that I explore in this book is based on the variety of discussions and debates I have had over my 20 years of training, managing and leading others. Many of these people stand out in my mind right now. They made me better and for so many reasons. While they may have gained from me, I feel I have gained so much more from them.

I must also acknowledge my peers. Trainers are an interesting group. They live to be in front of a group and create a forum of growth and development. They work towards the one or two things which will make someone's job just a little bit easier.

Some of these trainers are very serious, methodical trainers. Some are rather adlib kind of folk who let the nature of the discussion direct the learning experience. Others are simply facilitators of a PowerPoint. There have been story tellers, instigators, pontificators, debaters and teachers. Some have so large an ego; it can be hard to imagine anyone else in the room except them and their gargantuan cranium. And others just simply want to give of themselves to the art of training. I thank each and every one for the lessons learned. For I believe each has a lesson to learn.

I have had the benefit of many mentors during my professional career. They have been in the world of training and in the world of management. They have been owners, vice-presidents, regional supervisors, store managers and sales people. Sometimes it took place in a ten-year career with a men's fashion corporation or a three-hour dinner talking about retention and adoption or a two-minute interaction with a customer service agent. Part of my goal for this book is to be a bit of a mentor as a gesture to give back.

Lastly, one cannot exist without the family and friend network. My Dad is a barometer of a stand-up businessman. He is now retired and when he was working, he always exemplified the best of any work ethic you could define. My wife is the best manager I have ever known. She modeled so much of what is important in being a strong manager. She is now a stay-at-home mother and works twenty-times harder than I ever will. Do I use these as sources for the book? How could I not? They shaped my life and my desire to share with and grow others.

INTRODUCTION

Inevitably, I will be training a topic and a learner will ask, "Yeah, but what if this happens?" I don't mind. In a way, I expect this to take place. As counter-intuitive as this may sound, it is planned improvisation. This word, improvisation, is very important to the soul of this book. Nothing in life is scripted, especially when getting things done through others.

What is the very nature of a "What If" situation? It is when the manager faces an unexpected aspect of their job and has to make a decision. It can be that moment in a situation where you have to act while sometimes feeling a degree of uncertainty with a variety of possible actions. It can also be a proactive moment as you contemplate action associated with a task yet to be started. These moments force you to react or consider possible reactions. You have to improvise and think on your feet. You may not like it. You may have to react in a certain way because other options do not seem available.

Let's say it is a Tuesday and you have just come into work. You are in your office doing some operational paperwork. A team member bursts in demanding you deal with the other team member who is driving them 'nuts'. You did not get the memo for this. In this and in most situations, there are three absolutes. One, you now have to face the **UNKNOWN**. This would relate to the team member coming in that you did not plan and the issue of the 'nuts' comment. It is composed of things with which you have absolutely no perspective, yet. Two, you have a series of things you **NEED TO KNOW** to do something. This would be the required perspective from the team member, the facts behind the issue and some ideas for action. It represents as much information gathering as possible. And three, there is **WHAT YOU NOW KNOW** to guide your way. This is the action you make based on what is uncovered regarding the team members, the nature of the situation and the possibilities. Whether these things are perceived as exciting or scary, these things are what make successful managers rise above the rest.

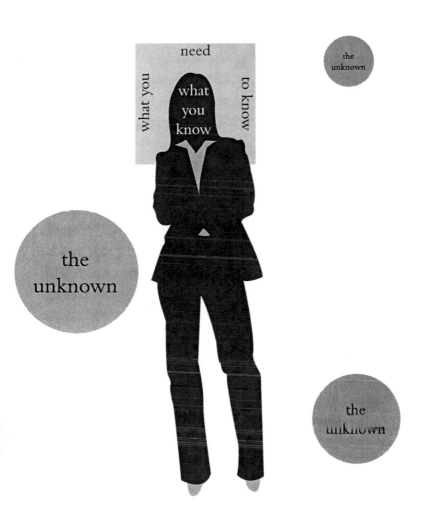

Your awareness as manager will support your next step.

In a way, it is awareness which drives all actions as managers. It can be the awareness of the people or the situation. It can be the awareness of the company and the policies which dictate action. It can be your awareness of who you are and your biases. Improvisation cannot exist without awareness. Sounds like a formula, right?

There are formulas in business. Managers desire to have a one-size fits all, default answer to this or that in managing, leading, directing, influencing and so on. Managers want the "A + B = C" formula to deal with all things. The problem is, this can be limiting, stereotypical or biased and too rigid. This static formula does exist and may apply, but there is nothing static about managing people. It will always contain variables. You must change your lens, your viewpoint, your mindset. The only equation that fits is the flexible formula "A + Variables = Customized Approach". The more effective approach is one of adaptation or improvisation.

The "A" represents the constants in management. They are the things in the business which must happen. In many ways, these are the day-to-day operations of the business. For example: making sales, training your team, putting out the inventory and following up with the client.

The "Variables" represent the unknown and sometimes uncontrollable things making up the day. This relates to the unplanned elements of the day. For example: A team member's motivation, a system breaking down unexpectedly, a client's reaction to something or anyone's relative understanding of what is happening right then.

The "Customized Approach" represents the action to achieve the goal ("Constants") based on the context of what is happening ("Variables"). This decided-upon approach is the improvisational response to getting things done in general and through others. Managers must release any pre-conceived notions to control things in one particular way or method to solve things. The key is to embrace the power of flexibility needed to be successful in today's diverse, complex and ever-changing environment.

To provide context, think of one of your policies. Some one is non-compliant regarding that policy. Do you have a "three strikes, you're out" response? This would be the "A ∣ B = C" formula. And while it might make sense to follow a rigid path, do variables exist within the context of the situation which might lead to another path or course of action? For example, is the non-compliance a lack of understanding or ability? Did an obstacle prevent the compliance?

These answers play a part. This would be the flexible formula "A + Variables = Customized Approach". Notice the policy ("A") is still important and ultimately the goal. It is the Variables which provoke a more relative and relevant managerial action.

To be fair, I know there may be a few managers who disregard the idea of hypothetical discussion. They are uneasy speaking about what has not occurred or what may happen. The argument may be that everyone will react to a situation differently and no on really knows how they may act. So, how can you really speculate? This is the reason to discuss the hypothetical. Be proactive and think about possible situations and ask "What If"? Then begin working through the possibilities to be better prepared for thinking on your feet based on a foundation of best practices. This is the book. It is designed to offer insight into being improvisational. The goal is to develop a think on your feet mindset. Why? Because I have seen too many well intentioned managers want some type of crafted answer for the thing that is in front of them. What I mean by that is, stuff happens and managers want one size fits all. They then struggle with making the "square peg" fit into the "round hole". In this book, you will be introduced to elements of being a successful "What If" manager.

The following chapters will do this. Chapter one will define what it is to embrace the unknown. This will involve embracing something unplanned. Chapter two will provide a review of various situations. It is meant to provoke both awareness and reflection of what to do. This promotes a proactive understanding of common things occurring in management. Chapter three looks at adopting this new mindset and skill set based on working with what you now know. It will clarify simple activities to sustain this improvisational energy.

Let me make this perfectly clear. It is impossible to provide concrete answers to the topics provided in the book. Here is why – "A + Variables = Customized Approach". I can picture a manager reading this book and asking "So what is the answer?" It depends. Ask questions. Consider the possibilities. My intent is to provide a basis for thinking on your feet, to provide an awareness of what is important when making decisions as manager when you face the unplanned.

Have fun looking at being improvisational. Explore the things that may, might, can and will most likely occur. Begin planning for the unplanned.

Simply put,
life is unscripted.

Chapter One

The Unknown

An improvisational management style or thinking on your feet style must first embrace that "stuff happens". Plan all you want, something will interfere. A reality in managerial success is to acknowledge this. Before learning the skill of improvisation, you must begin with an awareness of this skill. You must orient the mindset and the action will follow.

We will look at two distinct considerations in this chapter. The first consideration is the nature of the unknown. Think about that one. It dictates that you will never know if it is large or small, people or process, or whatever. And yet as manager, you

are required to react to a changing landscape based
your relative awareness and overall abilities. It is
the not knowing which confounds most managers.
When people do not have all the facts, they fill in the
blanks based on their own relative understanding.
Or they wait. Does waiting help or hinder the situation? These thoughts represent an important aspect
in orienting your mindset; to not know and still do
something.

The second is the nature of improvisation and
it's presence in a management style. The idea is to be
proactive in being reactive. I bet you will re-read that
sentence. I would too. Stuff happens and we must do
something when that stuff occurs even or especially
if we do not plan for it. At this point we sort through
a variety of options on how to act. To be improvisational is to have a previously considered number of
actions "in your back pocket" to use in select situations. This library of actions is foundational in nature
with the ability to flex and adapt to meet the needs
of the situation. You must rely on your own abilities
to act.

In my experience, I have shared some time with
managers who hold on very rigidly to a need to control everything going on around them. In major or
even minor unexpected events, the managers would

be fearful or overwhelmed. The very things making up their comfort zone were no longer there. Adjustments were being suggested, or more oft than not, demanded and these managers simply had a very difficult time adjusting. In this instance, acknowledgement of the first consideration would be to accept not having all the facts does not make you a poor manager. Control freaks can be perfectionists. The acknowledgement of the second consideration would be to always plan for issues or unplanned situations and have some contingencies.

To the contrary, I have also met those who were too laid back needing a major scenario to wake them up. In some cases, it wasn't due to their being laid back, but rather not being held accountable. Lack of accountability is an effect created by so many potential causes within a manager's reality. It could be a lack of leadership, systems which do not track or measure performance, responsibilities not clearly defined or trained, or an absence of vision creating apathy. The first consideration would be to investigate the root cause and the second would to have planned responses to each possible root cause.

In either case, consider the scope of all which must be done in a given day. What is important and what is trivial? When things happen, managers are sometimes asked to react to things with which they do not necessarily agree, or care about or more importantly, did not plan to have to deal with at that moment. Which gets the attention? What is driving your choice? It, being choice, is based on one's motivation. Motivation is about decisions people make for themselves. Think about what is influencing the choice. To think on your feet means to choose to do something. Ultimately, any choice is based on a degree of value for the situation. Is it accurate or fair?

Relax; you are not alone in this day-to-day managerial or leadership reality. Things happen and you must do something. Even if you know all the data or choose plans of action that back-fire, this thinking on your feet is about action-reaction. It is about taking the information at the time and deciding a course of action. While improvisation is about reaction, I would suggest knowing the possibilities in a potential situation allows for some determination of action. Think about this book as a means to review proactive decision making prior to your being in a reactive environment. By considering what may occur and what course of action may be best, you begin to create an improvisational mindset.

Someone, somewhere, is sitting in their workspace engaged in a situation and wondering about how to handle "this thing". They just want an answer or validation or insight into the extent of their next step. They want to just know what to do.

FOR EXAMPLE

A usually upbeat and capable team member is starting to suffer in performance. When you ask what is going on, they share they are having issues at home.

After review of a team member's effort to complete a task, you notice several mistakes. You know they tried their very best and it was below standard.

Your branding has just changed. Sell the concept to your team.

Your day has been filled with reactionary stuff and you are behind on your tasks. Your loved one calls and asks if you can come home early today to help out.

So what if this happens, what do you do?

ACTIVITY

Without lifting your pen or pencil, connect all the dots using only four lines.

•   •   •

•   •   •

•   •   •

Answer on page 78

CHAPTER TWO

WHAT YOU NEED TO KNOW

So why do the exercise? It represents your situations. Are you looking intentionally at it? Did you solve it without pecking? In this chapter, you will need to consider the improvisational skills associated with managing, leading, inspiring, directing and getting things done without answers. The goal is to be aware how possibilities drive action.

In the following pages, we will look at a series of select management topics. While insight will be shared, your awareness of the issues represents the source of learning. The experience will involve both reflection and considerations. Each situation will have a key thematic point to reflect upon. As for context, think about your own experiences. If you are part of a group of managers, look at the opportunity to discuss your experiences and role-play as to how to navigate the situation.

Why? Think of athletes. They endure hours, days and a tremendous amount of time studying and practicing their sport and, more specifically their position and all its respective responsibilities. Then, there is an intense focus on all of their impact to the team dynamic. Overall, an enormous amount of energy, effort, blood, sweat and tears are given to their craft. These efforts are designed to prepare the mind and body to react to any situation.

Like athletics, management is fluid and ever-changing at a moment's notice. It is most often unique and framed by the circumstances, or context of the situation. The best way to prepare for the unknown is to practice the most common scenarios by using an established foundation of the most adaptable and flexible best practices.

Thinking on your feet is perhaps best explained by two questions; "What if this happens?" and "What if I (you) do this?" These are key questions to work through as manager. The first question promotes an awareness that anything can happen, while the second promotes a willingness to do something. This is improvisation.

And then there is the third question to ponder; "What if policy dictates an action?" This can be a struggle. I believe managers know anything can happen and in most cases feel very confident they can figure it out. A company policy can challenge the very heart of improvisation. Managers may fear their decision versus what the company has defined. Which perspective is the one that is the most relevant and makes the most sense for the individual, team or business?

Regardless of what you may face in your role as manager, regardless of any given context, as well as all policy considerations, there are foundational elements which will always apply. Something happens. It is unplanned. What matters next is how you respond. The key is in how you look at the situation; think improvisational lens. Improvisation is the act of looking intentionally at all situations. This is you looking at the situations you will face in an effort to know more. This is necessary to do something in reaction. Understand a difference. This is not seeing intentionally as that is passive. Looking requires active participation. A participation which will always include a review based on common factors.

What are some of the most common factors for engaging in improvisational management?

PAY ATTENTION. It is OK to stop, look and listen. In fact, it is imperative to pay attention to your senses. Not so much to taste or smell, but you get the picture. Often there is a sixth sense, your "gut". This awareness does not originate from a physiological source or nervous system. It comes from the perceptions and decisions made through life's experiences. Is it OK to rely on your instinct? Yes. Is it OK to decide to do something without all the information or data supporting the moment? Yes. While this type of flexibility may cause some managers to flinch, the saying goes, "it is better to beg forgiveness, than to beg permission." Work your senses and be very aware. It promotes movement towards action/reaction.

PERSPECTIVES. In any given situation, there will be your perspective. There will probably be another perspective as well. It could be the company, your boss, a peer or someone else involved in the situation. Knowing a complete perspective is to know a broader view. This may involve asking a few questions before acting. The push back may be time. How much does time really impact action? At the minimum, a manager must rely on their own perspective to make a decision. Managers have been tasked to get things done, especially through others. They must act. If management and improvisation implies action, it also implies you have to act with or without all the perspectives in place.

IT DEPENDS. This is the biggest challenge for managers. Context is everything in life. Nothing in life is without a cause–effect. Nothing in life is without relevance to something else. Nothing in life is without some type of contributing factor shaping that moment in time. Therefore, a static formulaic approach is problematic.

Think about something simple like coming to work late. You may have a policy about this issue. What if one team member has been late several times, another top performing team member has only had one instance and another has had two times over six months with additional issues as well, do you respond in the same manner with each? In your job, there will be times when you have to adapt and be flexible in your degree of managing a situation. Be careful. This is not to suggest everyone is held to a different standard. Not at all, a standard is a standard. It is to suggest, what you do in an effort to maintain a fair and equitable standard will depend on the team member, the situation and the context surrounding both.

COMMIT TO SOMETHING. Improvisation implies an act of doing; a "just do something" mentality. It is like the famous statement by the Jedi Master, Yoda, "Do or do not, there is no try." This statement proclaims to do or even not to do commits to action, while to try is passive. Now, to be improvisational means you must have some room and power to navigate options and then act. Nothing stifles improvisation more than being capable, but not able. I have found a challenge for improvisation tied to the level or degree of authority to decide a course of action. Managers may not know the extent of their own empowerment. This may sabotage the manager from being improvisational. This lack of boundaries can keep improvisation in check. And even if the decision is to do nothing (which can be a viable decision in the right context), be sure to tell the team member or members, that is your decision.

So how does all this work? The following pages will share common topics in management. They will provide enough understanding for you to think "yeah, I deal with that". However, it is virtually impossible for me to share the exact answer for each topic as it applies to you. What might work within retail may have little or no application in manufacturing or hospitality. So consider how these topics might manifest themselves within your reality. Then explore potential "What If" possibilities and your improvisational response to them.

Based on the improvisational common factors, look intentionally at each of the following topics and your potential "What If" and ask yourself:

Based on the situation within the topic,

- What is the look, sound and feel of this situation?

- What do the perspectives tell you about this situation?

- What aspects of the situation impact your options?

- What things would you be willing to commit to do?

Two.1 **ACCOUNTABILITY**

This may be the first and hardest test for a manager — to hold someone accountable for something
within the business. It is one thing to allow people
to make mistakes. It is yet another to allow for unacceptable performance or behavior and be held hos-
tage as manager. What is driving this decision? Many
times it is associated with a desire to avoid conflict
or to be liked. Being liked and getting the job done
causes much angst for some managers. Fun and discipline are not mutually exclusive to one another.
They just need the definition as to how each exists
within an organizational framework.

As with all jobs, it is important to be very clear
about performance and productivity expectations.
Connect with your team by scheduling ongoing
meetings. Sometimes your team does not know how
they are doing and this causes accountability issues.
And by the way, more times than not, the only time
a team member hears from a manager is when they
need to improve something. Be sure to share what
your team does well versus what they are not doing
well. Think of a ratio which is heavier to the positive
versus the negative.

While consistency and fairness are important, every team member has their own merits. They have a certain something unique to the team and business. Pay attention to that aspect of the relationship. To value the importance of the job is one thing. To value the relationship means getting to know what makes them tick, you tick and the team tick. Accountability is linked to both what is expected (the job) and why it matters (the team member).

Are you **willing** to let someone go for non-compliance to an expectation?

Two.2 **Buddy versus Boss**

One of the first tests and a testament to your leadership will be the transition from peer to the leader. Hypothetically, one day you were their peer and the next day you were their boss. Everyday which follows you have to build credibility as a boss. What you do will directly relate to how you establish your responsibility and what will be acceptable behaviorally. I am not suggesting you must be an enlightened despot or maniacal leader. I am stating you must create a sense of boundary, a scope of understanding and clarity for your team.

Think of an actor. They must play a part. When stepping on stage, they act well their part. Now when off the stage, they may act differently. It is the same for managers with a team of friends.

Also ask yourself, are you worried about being liked or respected? There is a difference. I may like you because you snowboard or have kids. Respect implies a provision of a sense of worth to someone based on their ethics, qualities or abilities. My father told me, as manager your goal is not to make friends but rather work hard and do the right thing to get the job done. That has always stuck with me. He was not opposed to making friends or having friends. He was sharing that friendship in the workplace is fine, just not the primary goal of a supervisor.

You must understand and believe why you were placed in that role. You must clarify the quality and degree of your relationships within the team. You must become very aware of the overall team environment and how performance will be measured.

You are now supervisor, be one.

Two.3 **Change**

Defining change is complicated. It can be so many things and mean different things to everyone on your team. And of all the topics in this book, this will be the hardest for me to share with you. While I cannot tell you what types of change you will encounter in the future, I can tell you that your team will look to you and your ability to position change with them and their job.

Consider the team. Your team will undoubtedly react to the change. They will start by becoming very aware of how you initially react to the change. Then they will think about what happens next and what the change will mean to them. It is these thoughts which impact the improvisational management style. Your choice of words, actions and next steps will impact how change is both perceived and adopted.

You must understand that any response to change will always be based on the degree in which one embraces, accepts, ignores or resists the change. It gets challenging since no one will ever be on the same page. You may have a mix within your team.

Now consider the organization and its history with change. In general, how is change viewed

within the organization? How much change has already occurred and will this be viewed as a sort of
flavor-of-the-month?

As you proactively look at change, develop a team
that looks at challenging the status quo and is always
exploring better ways. Acknowledge collaboration as
an effective tool to achieve new ideas and direction;
especially by making brainstorming ideas a part of
your general meeting structure. Also make it a habit
to give the team a new game to play as often as possible.

Change **is** inevitable.

Two.4 **Congruence**

This is another way of looking at ethics. Congruence may be seen as the act of coming together, or being of same mind, or being in agreement. The goal is to look at congruence as a meeting of the self and the job. In other words, are you true to yourself when making decisions and thinking on your feet about what needs to happen? Consider the reality of biases. I dare you to go into any situation without some type of bias. Do you view people, places and things without labels? It's impossible. We cannot evaluate a situation if we cannot judge it. Biases are necessary and do have a place in a situation. The key is to understand how they impact our decision making and if they are helping or hindering our ability to get the job done.

What if a bias is getting in the way? Identify if it is a professional or personal bias and why. I believe this to be a very big consideration. Think about how this bias impacts your decision. Think about the possibility if your decision will bother you at night. If your decision ended up in the company newsletter, would you feel good or bad? Managers will at some time question a decision based on who they are and what they believe. Therefore, will you find yourself rationalizing the bending of rules or shortcuts to meet a goal?

Emotions can be made up of opinions, which are subjective and biased in nature (not a bad thing, just problematic). And stay true to your beliefs. Too many managers change what makes them "them" in an effort to fit in or succeed. This can alter what originally made you successful.

Let truth
and
objectivity orient
your path.

Two.5 **Difficult Employee**

This is very tricky! First, why are you thinking this? Is your belief based on objectivity or subjectivity? Is the answer aligned with behavioral accountability or your perception of the individual? Second, why are difficult employees difficult? Think like the team member. Perhaps they think their choices are the most effective way and have worked for them in the past. Now what about the manager? Perhaps the manager allowed this or felt fear about addressing it. Consider the possibility that both parties may very well have created this unacceptable behavior.

Difficult is relative until it can be defined. The main way to define difficult is through behavior. For example, you may have a team member who is quick to say "It's not my job." Really? In a split second ask yourself if the responsibilities required and expected have been clearly defined and communicated. Then ask the team member about their awareness of the situation. That alone might impact everything. Then begin to analyze the extent of the situation. This may involve how much or how long this has been an issue, their overall performance, other contributing factors or that they may be completely unaware of their boundaries or the consequences of their actions.

Ideally, when working with a difficult person, consider all potential perspectives. The goal is to learn more and to understand. As a means to explore alternative viewpoints, switch roles. Ask them "what would you do if you were manager and...?" This activity will make them accountable for the decision and outcome. You may even see a new perspective of how you manage and lead.

Never assume.
Ask questions.

Two.6 **Discipline**

This is one of the most misunderstood concepts. It is widely used in an immensely negative connotation. It is important for managers to know that discipline is about creating boundaries, ensuring healthy environments and saving people. Most managers assume discipline is only about firing people. Firing people is easy and takes about 5 seconds, providing you have done a bunch of other things correctly to support the team member. This inherently implies you have some type of performance management cycle required in an effort to get people back on track and to help them.

Identify whether or not this is an actual issue and, if so, what brought it about? Does the situation conflict with policy or is it personal? Then ask your self a series of questions regarding training, follow-up, coaching, follow-up, measurement and more follow-up. If you send someone away due to lack of support, whose fault is it?

When you begin to add structure to a think on your feet process, be sure to ensure objectivity. While things like documentation may be seen as additional paperwork, it is a necessary component of discipline.

Detail all action plans, desired outcomes and potential consequences. Show how you intend on supporting the development and be sure to clarify what will happen with improvement or continued substandard performance. Never threaten an action on which you are not willing to follow through. If you said you would do something, do something.

Discipline is not
about firing people,
it is about
saving people.

Two.7 GOALS

You may be part of an organization that creates goals very easily. They may execute goals from some type of pre-designed system. Maybe you are "old school" and have to establish individual and team goals on your own. You may call upon spreadsheets, a calculator or perhaps just good guessing. Regardless, these tasks are not so improvisational. In fact, the team want the facts here more than anywhere else as this aligns with their performance and how this impacts their value to the organization

Do you really know the goals, how they are made and why they are what they are? Does the organization establish them, do you know how and why? If you establish them, do you clearly understand what the business needs and what the end-user (client) needs? These questions need to be asked and answered. The answers you provide will factor in any improvisational reaction to a team member asking "Why this number, how much am I really off or who made these?" While you do not improvise the numbers, you do improvise the reactions to them.

When it comes to setting goals, analyzing goals and sharing goals, think transparency. No one on your team should ever guess how they are doing. Think of a sports team. Every player knows their stats at any given time. The coach's job is to analyze these stats and align how the player's performance impacted the results. This is a key to goals and goal setting. The goal will always be just a number. The effort to achieve the number is what managers need to figure out. As manager, you set goals, review them and re-set them. In between is where the thinking on your feet occurs.

Establish goals by individual, explain why, track them and post the results.

Two.8 **HYGIENE**

Can you think of a more personal issue? The first response you may have in reading this is "Is this about if someone stinks?" Yes, it could, but in what manner? It could be body odor, breath or extensive perfume. No matter which one, it is not personal, it is business. This is the mindset you must have – think about how this situation might affect the nature of the business.

Be realistic and professional. Do not sugar coat the situation. This is about being empathetic with a direct tone towards a specific goal. Then move toward ensuring the accuracy of the issue. How strong would you classify the issue (i.e. scent)? How much of this issue involves the client or team? If policy dictates a particular path of action, pay attention to what the policy requires. Then align how you would work with the team member to comply with the requirements.

On a more personal note and one of respect, be sure to keep the meeting private. The minute the conversation becomes apparent, the team member will react. Their reaction will probably be one of embarrassment or defensiveness (or both). If you think about their perspective, they may be OK with the feedback because perhaps they never knew. Therefore your mindset will be one of asking if there is anything you can do to support and help with the issue. Also NEVER ask if this a medical issue or element of ethnicity (culture). If it becomes evident, let them tell you this. Do not ask!

Despite this being a personal issue, it is not personal. It is business.

Two.9 **INSPIRATION**

Managers struggle to manage the "M" word. Are you good at motivation? Or are you good at clarifying expectations, training skills, coaching efforts and acknowledging choices in an effort to replicate behavior? You see, it is very difficult and near impossible to motivate someone else. Motivation is about personal choice. That is the key; someone else makes choices based on their own motivation. The best you can do is to inspire or give insight into making that choice. The emphasis must change from "trying to motivate" to "trying to inspire and influence a choice". They may seem the same. One seeks an end result while another seeks understanding.

When you find your self second guessing motivation, ask "Have you ever been told to do something but not told how?" Was that motivation or capability? People have specific goals, aspirations and interests that matter to them. Did you uncover what was important to the team member, their preferred style of feedback or the best way to support the individual? The importance of getting a bearing on their mindset and their needs is paramount. This influences how you communicate, coach, direct, influence, etc.

When establishing expectations or standards, clarify the why behind all things. Define the how involved in getting things done to ensure capability. Share all efforts and resources to support them in their job. Accentuate what they do by consistently and constantly providing acknowledgement for their job.

Motivation is not about forcing "it" to happen, it is about learning why "it" matters to others.

Two.10 NEW OR FIRST DAY

One of the most anxious things team members endure is being new to the company and being held accountable to new expectations. This becomes even more challenging when there are very specific objectives and core values linked to a clearly defined vision and set of guiding principles. Being the "new guy or new gal" means learning a new way to do things. Think about that first. What is the mindset of the new team member? What is shaping their next steps? Ask what expectations they have about the company, the job and you as manager.

If you had 30 seconds, what would you say to someone new about your organization? Can you imagine that the new team member may place an equivalent amount of importance on anything and everything you say? You must establish what is critical, what is secondary and what is of lesser importance. This tiered approach allows for things to proceed little by little, as opposed to an overwhelming mass.

Be sure to be clear and let the team member know exactly what you want and need them to do. Make it realistic and help them to understand what will occur during their day. Clarify the expectations within the scope of their responsibilities. Focus on the objective and clarify how it will be measured. Ensure they know the extent of your growth-oriented environment where development is constant and ongoing.

Be empathic. Let them know they matter and are valued as an important part of a team.

Two.11 **Perfection**

Some people like to claim they are perfectionists. Their intent behind this belief is that successful people are somewhat perfectionist in their efforts to get the job done. To work towards perfection is not an issue. The difficulty is that nothing in life is perfect. The job, the people and the very tasks are innately imperfect, which creates difficulties for a perfectionist.

What about the other side of the coin? Imagine a team member who does not seek perfection, but feels they work in a perfectionist environment. They struggle with their confidence. They make mistakes while others excel. Their performance will be affected by this viewpoint. This may be a valuable employee with a confidence issue.

Either way, ensure the clearly defined responsibilities live in an environment where mistakes are OK. Does the support of the manager include training and coaching or is it just the "get it done" policy that drives action? If any consequences are involved, how are they defined? Is there a depth of feedback regarding recognition and reconstruction of behavior?

The key is to set realistic and attainable goals for everyone. Make things win-able. This builds confidence. Then move to bigger challenges. Always celebrate wins. Be a rewarding manager with the goal of giving praise openly and often. Also experiment with standards of success. Investigate different ways to do things. Allow for creativity and experimentation.

Make learning from successes and mistakes a positive thing.

Two.12 **PERFORMANCE**

As a new manager, you may very well understand the importance of hitting targets. You probably hit your targets to an extent which landed you in the job as manager. Now you are required with making sure your team hits their targets and that their performance is at or exceeds expectations. Do you struggle with knowing some team members hit their numbers better than others and then assume why? That is the challenge. You very rarely worry about the performers, except that they continue performing. Your biggest concern is the ones who do not perform to targets or expectations. The even bigger concern is why. This is one of the reasons improvisation attached to a number is so difficult.

Managing performance means understanding the range of reasons why someone is not performing to expectation. Thinking on your feet will always require you to do your research and analyze degrees of performance. Is this a trend or is this a one time thing? Also review whether this team member has been fully trained. If the answer is no, have you defined what is fully trained. You may need to self-assess just how much coaching, feedback and instruction you have provided and how often. And lastly, explore if there are any external influences.

Your objectivity will be important when analyzing and reviewing numbers. Seek trends not absolutes. And do not wait until the end of the month for analysis. Have a meeting upon review and brainstorm the situation. Ask "why, how and what can we do". Isolate cause and work on what may be influencing their behavioral choice; like their abilities, knowledge, systems, or willingness. Be supportive and work on the skill.

Numbers are the result of a behavioral choice.

Two.13 **Personal Conflict**

There is no guarantee that we will like the people with which we work. In fact, more common than not, the reality is we may not like the person that works with us. The issue is sometimes "I don't like you" and other times it can be "My job is affected because of you." In addition, competition may exist in some fashion. Conflict can be based on biases, perceptions and attitudes.

If the manager is part of the conflict, think, "I will manage the behavior, not the attitude." This is where you really need to adapt or be flexible. You may want to address the attitude. If you argue attitude, it will be a "ping pong" game. This is based on an opinion or perception. While an attitude may be perceived as the issue, there will always be something being done behaviorally that causes that perception. Managing the behavior is a better approach.

If the manager is outside the conflict and must be involved, the first step will always be to get as much data as possible behind the situation before acting. Collect all pertinent resources, define the situation and then act. To ensure accuracy, verify your understanding of the situation and the needs of others.

While it may be easy to get caught up in the personal vs. professional boundaries being shared with the team, stay objective. Set rules and guidelines for communication in conflict. Make it known feedback will be shared and therefore create an agreement that each party will respect the conversation. Establish listening rules; one person speaks at a time. Relationships must always be the priority. Brainstorm ideas to improve the relationship and situation; always remained focused on strengthening the relationship. Agree to a next step, even if complete resolution is not planned and even if it means helping someone out of the team.

The key to the success of managing personal conflict is respect for the individual and the business.

Two.14 **Personal Issues**

How far do you go to be manager? How far into someone's life do you manage or lead? You are tasked to oversee your team and the efforts to get the job done. You also oversee the behaviors brought to the job. Like it or not, the personal equation plays a part in the professional experience. You will bring "some thing" (e.g., viewpoint, problem, issue, etc.) to work, therefore it is obvious to assume the team will do the very same. This can be tricky. Be aware of how this will play out.

If you face any issue, what you manage must be associated with behavior; especially behaviors involved in the business. This dictates to have facts as they pertain to the job. Think of someone who brings a scowl to work or an abruptness to their communication. Are you managing based on your opinions or observable facts? If in doubt or if you have a hunch, uncover the nature of the issue by asking if there are any other contributing factors. You may find this may have nothing to do with you or the business. However, in more serious situations, there may be some type of HR, organizational policy or support available (or required).

If you find yourself in this situation, never as-sume. Ask questions and clarify the context of the situation. Be supportive no matter what the situation. A manager must always air to the mindset of "what can I do to support you in this situation?" Be upfront about what the business needs. Establish very clearly, as it pertains with action and time lines, what you need to have happen in the situation. In some cases, ask, "Are you willing to...?" They have to give you a sense of what they are or are not willing to do. This allows you to know the big picture for next steps.

Ask what is best for the business? Does this situation matter to the business?

Two.15 **Scheduling**

Nothing is more living and breathing in management than a team schedule. It seems that no matter how much you proactively plan, design, maneuver or tweak a schedule, it will change somehow. Even with the best intentions, your team will challenge your choice of schedule.

At the heart of this situation is the question, how legitimate is this change or the need for the new schedule? One of the first considerations falls on the one who wants to change the schedule. Have other options been investigated before the request? Also does this same party know what accommodations must be made or the general understanding of what this change is causing? Whenever changing a schedule, the best interest must be found for all team members. Also pay attention to whether this is a chronic or one-time situation.

Essentially, provide some established matter of policy. If this is a one-off situation, then improvise. If not, live by the standards. Stop for a moment. This book is about thinking on your feet. How can enforcing standards be improvisation? Simple, the standard does not flex, your abilities to work with the situations surrounding it do. Everyone must be held accountable to scheduling. A manager may have to adapt to make it work.

Team members must look at solving changes on their own first. Ensure they are looking at alternative ways to cover the shift before they come to you. Stand your ground and work towards resolution.

Acknowledge the needs for a schedule, support the structure of a schedule and have a plan when changing a schedule.

Two.16 **Sense of Urgency**

Managers will often have to work with an employee who seems to have a lack of urgency to get things done. This is a question of what, why and to what extent. It may be presumed to be a lack of motivation. While this is a valid claim, many managers don't analyze the reasons for the lack of urgency. It may be the effect of a lack of understanding of the business goal or urgency of task. It could be a lack of knowledge or information to make decisions. It may be tied to a lack of skill to successfully or properly accomplish a task. It may be a lack of buy in or that the priority of the task does not align with other assigned priorities. It could also be that they are not stimulated by the job or they are simply done with their tasks.

A manager's first goal is to "tag" it. This means call it out. Instead of ignoring your feeling, ask what is ultimately at the heart of this situation? Urgency is relative to both sender and receiver. As manager you are assured of at least one perspective, your own. Another perspective may be associated with how much the team members are challenged or stimulated with problem solving or creative thinking. Are expectations and boundaries set or established? Does any formal or lack of formal coaching impact their urgency? How often are each provided?

Be sure to create and maintain a platform for consistent and ongoing coaching. Never stop developing your team. When possible, solicit ideas from your team about select subjects. Have them brainstorm and provided insight. It is very important to both acknowledge the ideas and then use them in some way.

Have you let this occur due to your own influences to the team? Are they modeling you?

Two.17 **Stress**

Good luck not having some type of stress at one time or another when you manage others. Change can cause anxiety due to a lack of control. You may have to make a decision with a lack of data. You may be put into a place where your expectations do not match those of the organization. I dare you to not feel stressed. Do you think your stress goes unnoticed by those around you?

Reflect on some of these questions. Are you even aware of the extent of what it is that is being asked of you? Does what you are being asked to do have objective goals, detailed action and time lines? What about the concept of empowerment, the boundaries within your job and the realization that sometimes goals are unrealistic? Many times stress is associated with what is unknown, undefined or seeming out of the control of the manager.

If you find yourself stressed, the best improvisational next step is to breathe. It helps. Next, ask questions about the situation. Be sure to have a complete understanding of what it is you need to do. Also provide the same platform for your team members. Embrace the emotion. What someone feels right then and there is a natural reaction to change and anxiety. A very important next step is for you to own your feelings and share them. If stress is a reaction from your team, acknowledge them and provide an empathic tone.

Balance emotion (what you need) with action (what you need to do).

Two.18 **Talent**

When you lead others, especially talented others, you can expect the talented ones are highly motivated individuals. You must consider this and take into account their interests and unique characteristics. Managing talent is relationally-based leadership. Strong people follow you not because you are cool nor have a motivational pitch, but because they have tied value to the task or ideal regarding their job. Either they did it on their own or you created this. In any case, a good manager can tie the relationship of a goal with the unique interests and personal needs of the team member.

As in all coaching and development, identify what style of feedback will work best for each individual team member. Remember, the intent behind their actions will more than likely be those of initiative and resourcefulness. Be aware that there may be times when this initiative may create conflict with you or others. Even if their actions are in conflict with you, what is the positive side of this situation?

Always set a clear direction. Articulate the vision and help set the goals for the team with next steps. Never compare one team member to another.

Always compare performance to a target or expectation. Do not squish a team member regarding errors; they will happen. Share the boundaries within decision making. Make development and education a constant. This involves training, coaching, guiding and advising (ideally one-on-one).

Forget trying to motivate, they already are motivated. Encourage, stimulate and influence them.

Two.19 **Vulgarity**

OK, someone used inappropriate language. Inappropriate according to who or what? Was it "f-bombs", gender or racial slurs or was it just a poor choice of language? Either way, it can be problematic because it may offend someone. So why is any language situation a big deal? The first review must be regarding the importance of a professional environment. The second is maintaining a non-threatening work environment. What is or is not vulgar is associated with those elements.

What is vulgar or how should it be defined? Vulgar language by an individual usually denotes insecurity of the individual, a desire for attention, frustration or efforts to control or manipulate others. It is not the language on it's own as much as it is the intent behind it or how the language can impact a work environment. It is important to the team as well as the individual to know the boundaries of language.

Always ensure a pleasant work environment for all. Do not let your actions linger; tag the observed behavior immediately. Do not jump to conclusions or ignore situations; investigate as needed. This is very important with any "he said/she said" situations. Ensure all accuracy of facts. If serious in nature, contact supervisor and HR or someone within the organization designed to handle these types of situations.

Be honest and **direct** about the impact. Think "Cause-Effect".

Two.20 "You Never Told Me That"

Nothing is more frustrating as a manager than to deal with an issue whereby the excuse, response or challenge by the team member indicates they did not know the information in the first place. Who is at fault here? In some cases, it is the manager. In others, it may be a team member's desire to see how far they can go or to see if they are really being held accountable to this task. Another element may be that assumptions were made by both parties. The manager may think "I trained them, so I'm good." The team member may think "I hear you, I'm good." What was done after the training that confirmed understanding? Two sayings to contemplate, "If it is not written, it is not real" and "They said they understood so I guess they understand".

So, were expectations clearly defined? Was the team member trained? Was understanding verified? Was coaching and feedback provided? Did the team member show they were capable? Was measurement tracked and shared? Were consequences established for doing it or not doing it? OK, if "yes" is the answer to all of these, willingness is the issue.

In any task, be very clear about the following elements: Why (reasons to do it), How (methods to do it), Support (training and coaching to effectively do it) and Acknowledgement (reinforcement and reward for the doing of it).

Focus on the cause (behavior) and effect (result), not the person.

ACTIVITY

The topics painted a picture. That's it. The goal is now to look at each topic and explore what are some of the most common "What If" possibilities within each topic. Look intentionally at each topic. So whether it is just you or a group of managers, the mission or ideal is to reflect and decide what improvisational action is needed within each topic. Think about what you might or should do if "this" happens.

Select a topic and define a particular situation. You or the group paints a minimal picture given the topic. Then choose a potential behavior or reactionary stance given the situation. This represents the team member or team members and their relative behavior and state of mind to be associated with the situation.

For example, you decide to choose Difficult Employee. Define the situation, "you are launching a new sales process to be followed with all clients". Define the behavior, "this team member has challenged each and every new program in the past and their response is one of open negativity". What do you do?

Apply the improvisational lens by asking the following questions:

- What is the look, sound and feel of this situation?

- What do the perspectives tell you about this situation?

- What aspects of the situation impact your option?

- What things would you be willing to commit to do?

Be sure to vary the context and behaviors. Also practice the unknown and have one of the participants bring a behavior to the situation which is undisclosed or unexpected.

These activities can involve role-playing, brainstorming or creative thinking. A degree of imagination and proactive thinking is required. The goal is problem solving. These activities will create and enhance your library of things to do if this or that happens. Remember, practicing the hypothetical "it" now is better than practicing the real "it" as it happens.

Improved listening skills will not necessarily result in improved listening. We must apply these skills. We must be convinced that it pays to listen. The combination of desire (I want to listen), effort (I'm going to work at it), and skill (I know how to do it) will result in improved listening.

– Donald L. Kirkpatrick

Chapter Three
What You Now Know

You now have a new way of looking at an improvisational mindset and about thinking on your feet. Do not forget you have abilities and knowledge already. You were elevated to manager because you have of set of skills which portrayed you as capable to oversee a team, a business and the efforts to provide for both. By embracing being improvisational or looking intentionally at situations and combining this with an existing skill set, you create a much greater awareness within your job. The challenge is both practicing these new skills and ultimately applying the new skills. What will get in your way?

Imagine a manager reading this book. They feel compelled to try some of the tips. They know this involves change, and change creates anxiety. They also know it means working with old habits or in some cases, developing new ones. There may be some pressure in the workplace based on how peer managers and supervisors (who are not familiar with the book or ideas) perceive this new concept. The team may even wonder, "OK, so what seminar did you go to or what book is it now?" How do you react?

A very common question after a training session is "so what is it you want me to do tomorrow?" I love this question. Pay attention to the intent behind the question. A learner is only expressing their need for "that thing" they need to do right away and "that something" that will immediately impact their job. As a means to expand the discussion, I might respond with "what do you think you need to do?" I believe people just want some type of answer. And I have found time and time again, the answer is already within the learner. Some may call it common sense or instinct. Improvisation relies on a certain trust that right or wrong, now or later, big or small, you have the ability to make the decision.

Another perspective takes shape. When working with a client, group or organization, someone has invested money and time into a need by providing training. Whatever the entity, it wants a return on its investment. It wants the behavior or metric to be enhanced, changed or made more or less. The need is understandable. An investment of some kind has been made and now a want (or demand) of something in return is expected. A common reciprocal question is expressed "training was done, now what?"

It is important to pay attention to these questions and expectations. The next question for both parties must be "OK, so what comes next?" I immediately think of the principle called Ockham's Razor (a.k.a. Occam's Razor). It is the theory put forth by William of Ockham in the 14th Century who stated that when considering all explanations for a phenomenon, the simplest is the most preferred. Using this means focusing on some very simple, very transferable, very do-able things to apply.

First off, begin creating a library. What? Yes, begin collecting stories and bits and pieces of stories which can relate to situations. For example, if I am facing a situation where two team members are at odds with one another, I will collect information. I will collect the "who said what, what makes up the situation and what I did to resolve the situation". Then when a similar or closely related situation comes about, I draw upon this information and use it to think improvisationally. I will use the data from the past to work with the present; "I have faced this and this is what I learned...". The key will be to customize the action and reaction based on the context and behavior associated with what is happening.

Also, establish some type of ongoing discussion platform within the organization. Make it a rule when discussing a topic, a "what if this happens" is applied as a means to help decisions to be made. Consider brainstorming and role-playing. These are the ultimate collective and collaborative processes. Ask a question and, using a note taking device (i.e. pad board, white board, etc.) list responses. Begin discussing the comments and begin analyzing each, their impact and importance to the topic. Paint situational pictures. Assign roles to participants and work through the situation. Have the observers provide feedback on their perspective of "what was good, what could be done differently and did the situation have resolution?" Creative thinking and problem solving are both additional means to shift paradigms. Put something to the group that is not expected. For example instead of sales, place the focus on relationships. Pose a question about "what is important in any relationship?" and ask "What if this happens?"

and make notes. Then correlate how this information can also impact sales.

The best resource for input, feedback, thoughts and keeping on track is using some type of peer network. Your peers can relate to anything you may be doing and what you may have to go through. They get it. This makes them a great advisor. They will be able to challenge you. They will be able to hold you accountable. Sometimes even without knowing why, they will just understand you, the situation and how to deal with it. It is amazing to watch this type of camaraderie. This effort entails establishing a group of people to challenge one another. The number can be two, three or more managers principally in a relative market, with whom you can connect, share and use as a sounding board, network with and help as needed. As a plan, meet with them on a weekly or bi-weekly basis. Make it a breakfast or lunch gathering. By the way, you are probably doing this already, just not with being improvisational as your topic.

I have had people to share ideas with in my career. At times, they offered a piece of precious advice or insight. It was great to just have them around. In a select moment, I might sometimes feel as if they were looking over my shoulder, even if they were not physically there. I just thought about what they might say if I chose one thing over another. This would relate to the concept; "What would Lance or Jackie or Chris do?"

An old saying is "if you can't measure it, you can't manage it." So the question in improvisational management is "how do you measure the unknown?" You can't. The goal is the not the measurement of the "What If", it is the measurement of the results from the "What If". For example, you have a team member quit all of a sudden. Do you measure the emotions attached to the departure or the effectiveness of your scheduling process? What about the recruiting program and your contingencies to react in an "all of a sudden" kind of staffing crisis? Measurement will be hard to look at until you are in the situation. So the goal will be to establish a selection of measures that are important to the business. Know those numbers and then as situations begin to take shape, you have a benchmark. Put simply, measure first, deal with the situation and then measure again.

Consider some type of Employee Value Index. How much do you value a means for the team member to provide feedback and rate the organization? It seems the team members have an opinion on the how the manager or company is doing, but they are rarely asked their view. Many organizations with which I have worked use some type of questionnaire to create a forum for feedback from the team. They are scored based on things like communication, leadership, culture, performance, values and the perception of their own place within the organization. This is about measuring you.

The idea is to reinforce what you know. It means planning, scheduling, identifying and monitoring the things which both aid and support the adoption of behavior. In a way, if you have made the effort to learn, the least you can do is to try what has been learned. Whatever happens next, it will require discipline. Going back to the situation at the beginning of this chapter, maybe the manager who may be wondering what to do next needs to ask...

- What is the look, sound and feel of this situation?

- What do the perspectives tell you about this situation?

- What aspects of the situation impact your options?

- What things would you be willing to commit to do?

STARTING YOUR LIBRARY

Tomorrow morning as you start your day, make a list of possible things which may occur. Then list your potential responses.

At the end of the day, go back to the list. Review the accuracy and inaccuracy of both what happened and what you did in response.

Another option would be to identify an aspect of your job. This could be a specific task, a team member, a system, a client profile or an upcoming launch. List every possible thing or variable which may happen as it relates to that targeted aspect. Now begin listing your options on what you might do regarding the variable.

The idea is to begin planning improvisation. If interested, make this a daily or weekly exercise. Keep a journal by making note of the "What If" situations and the actualities in your decision making.

CONCLUSION

When I became manager, all my decisions were shaped by my filter, or my relative understanding of the situation based on my experiences. I cannot adequately express my many blunders, near-misses and reactionary gaffs due to my relative inexperience. Then I learned a couple of things.

I was asked the question, "What do you want someone to do with the book (or the information it provides)?" At first, my instinct told me it was about helping managers make better decisions. It sounds OK. Then I began to speculate, what does 'better' mean? I believe it is more than just one thing. It is a series of one thing. One thing is managers must face situations with a higher degree of awareness. It must be an awareness which provides understanding. It is paying attention to what is going on and the relative context of the situation. It is the effort by a manager who wants to look intentionally at the things which occur in their job.

Another thing is perspective. All decisions made "if this happens" will be based on some type of judgment criteria. What does your perspective of the data tell you? Whether it is a little or a lot, it is what drives action. A manager must look at who they are, what has occurred, what they know and then do something.

One other thing is the ever changing nature of managing and leading others. There is not just one way to communicate, coach, inspire and so on. And while there are static ways to look at managing, it usually involves a very linear policy or procedure. If you then add a person to this process, it can get tricky. Managers must be flexible, adaptable and improvisational.

The last thing is just do something. It may seem a bit risky to decide to act without all the information. Remember, the decision is not what is right and that's it. It is right for right now given the information. If you have taken time to get to know the situation and the context surrounding it, the act of deciding is simply a natural next step. Be OK with your decision.

So what do you personally gain from understanding improvisational management, knowing yourself, applying a more flexible, adaptable management style and then acting? To borrow a line from the book, "it depends". I have no idea what your goal was in reading this book. Plus the amounts of management situations you will encounter are too many to number and too many to describe. Not to mention all of the varied industries and their realities. The answers will need to come from you. The goal from my perspective as author is for the reader to walk away with having reviewed some possible situations and reflected upon some possible actions. Therefore to know what you know, to identify what you need to know and to embrace the unknown is better than not doing either.

I was training a manager's leadership course for a large Canadian corporation. It was the first year of deploying the intensive, company-wide multiple-day course. I was delivering to my third or fourth group of managers and we were discussing causality. Specifically, we were discussing the analysis of statistics by defining that numbers were a result of behavioral choice. And I received the same question as I had in the previous groups, "Yeah, but what if this happens?" It struck me that this question is a reality for all managers. The unknown or the need to know is how managers live and lead. So we created a whole day of improvisational discussion, brainstorming and interaction. Best practices were shared and the learners all said their favorite part of the training was the act of looking at what to do in a "What If" situation. It gave them confidence. Confidence to be managers. We are now in the third year of adoption and "What If" is part of the training culture.

My hope is that the information in this book allows for all kinds of growth and introspection. It will not be the same for everyone. I am OK with that. Good luck and most of all, be flexible, adaptable and improvisational.

Answer to the activity on page 14

start

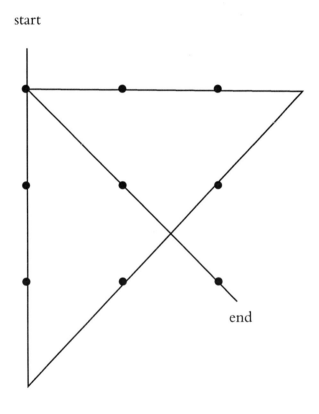

end

Kurt Reinhart is a teacher of managers. He has been working with businesses as a trainer-consultant for the past twelve years and has been professionally engaging teams of people for the last twenty plus years. Kurt oversees Create Training & Consulting with the mantra to define for his learners, "what is it you want me to do tomorrow?" He lives in beautiful Colorado and has an awesome wife with three great children.